SOPHIA OF THE BIBLE

Sophia of the Bible
THE SPIRIT OF WISDOM

*Sophia is the Greek word for Wisdom in the
original Greek of the Bible*

Interpreted and Compiled
by
Aurora Terrenus

Celestial Communications
The Publishing House of The Holy Order of Wisdom, Santa Cruz, CA

This book is dedicated to
the Spirit of Sophia
in You.

Aurora Terrenus

Celestial Communications is The Publishing House of The Holy Order of Wisdom, a non-profit organization dedicated to communicating and spreading the idea of the Spirit of Holy Wisdom for the enlightenment, enrichment, peace and prosperity of all.

Contents

Passages taken from these
Books of the Bible

Old Testament

Genesis	*Psalms*
Exodus	*Proverbs*
Job	*Ecclesiastes*

Old Testament Apocrypha

(Book of Wisdom)	*(Book of the Church)*
Wisdom of Solomon	*Ecclesiasticus*

New Testament

St. Mark	*I Thessalonians*
St. John	*Hebrews*
I Corinthians	*James*
Ephesians	*I John*
Philippians	*Jude*
Colossians	*Revelation*

It seems as if in the holy books of every great religion or philosophy there is an expression of magnanimous Love for Wisdom. In the eloquent poetic prose of The Holy Bible, *from the first book of Genesis, to the last book of Revelation, including the Apocrypha (which actually means 'from the secret, hidden'), she appears.*

From beginning to end, like the thread woven into a tapestry, she weaves in and out of Biblical history and yet is always there. She is the thread that connects and holds together the magnificent tapestry of Love. When the tapestry is turned and shown, she is Wisdom.

More dazzling in her brilliance than any constellation, she is the adoration of the wise. Never has one, who has seen her, not fallen in love with her beauty; for he who loved and loves her foremost, is God, is Love.

Who is she, this eternal Queen of Heaven,
this mirror of Love? Can she be the
embodiment of Wisdom, Sophia? There are
many great and scholarly interpretations of the
Bible, in which she is Wisdom. This is the first
interpretation of the Bible by a poet and
philosopher (lover of Wisdom) in which
Wisdom is Sophia.

All the passages about Sophia are not
included; study your Bible for others. The
passages that are included in this inter-
pretation are included to complete the
idea of Sophia, as the holy feminine spirit.
This symbol of perfection is the most precious
spirit the world could now know, love and
honor.

Book I

Introduction to Sophia

Proverbs
4:4-9

Treasure these words in your hearts:

Sophia is above all things.
Seek Sophia and become wise.
Know Sophia and she will keep you safe.
Love Sophia and she will comfort you.
Embrace Sophia and she will make you great.
Sophia will give you the golden crown
of beauty, grace, and glory.

Proverbs
8:1-12

Does not Sophia cry to us?
And when we have understanding,
do we not hear her voice?
Sophia stands at the highest
pinnacle on the mountaintops.
All ways and paths to the divine
illumination of Wisdom lead by her
to her heights.

Sophia weeps at the gates of
the entrance to the city:

"O children, to you I call.
That my voice might reach you
and the children of your children.
You, who are unknowing,
can know Sophia.
You, who are fools,
can become wise.

Hear me, because I speak
of exalted things.
From my lips come words
of the greatest glory.

My word is Truth.
All of my words are of the spirit,
pure and noble.
My words are self-evident
to the wise.
My words are true to those
who find knowledge.

Welcome my teachings more than silver.
Welcome my knowledge more than gold.

Sophia is more precious than rubies;
And of all things in the world,
to be desired, there is nothing
more worthy than Sophia.

I, Sophia, am Wisdom."

Proverbs
8:14

"I am a counsel of true Wisdom.
I am Understanding.
I have strength and power."

Proverbs
8:17–21

"I love those that love me.
Those that seek me shall find me.
Riches and honor are my gifts; yes,

gifts that are unsurpassable.
My gifts, my fruits, are of more
value than lustrous silver or pure gold.

I lead the way to Truth,
by the most discriminating intellect.
I exalt those that love me and
fill them with my treasures."

Proverbs
8:22-26

"The Lord and I, Sophia,
were together, in the beginning,
before time began.

We were together,
before his works of old.
We are the everlasting,
from the beginning,
before the earth ever was.

When there was nothing;
no hills, no mountains,

no water, no earth;
I, Sophia, was there."

Proverbs
8:27-35

"I, Sophia, was there
when the heavens were prepared.
I, Sophia, was there
when the compass to the depths
was placed on the face of the earth.

I, Sophia, was there
when the clouds were established.

I, Sophia, was there
when the fountains
of the deep were strengthened.
I, Sophia, was there
when the foundations
of the earth were appointed.

Then I was with him, co-creator,
separate and one with him.

I was daily his joy,
preceding and leading him,
always rejoicing.

On the earth,
I rejoice with the children
of our children.

Come to me, my children,
that I may bless your ways.
Know me and be wise.
I will bless those that hear me.

Whoever finds me,
finds life and
shall dwell forevermore
with Love and Wisdom."

Book II

Search for Sophia

Ecclesiasticus
24:34

Truly, my heart and soul search for Sophia
has not been for myself alone, but
for all seekers of Sophia.

(The Book of Wisdom)
The Wisdom of Solomon
1:6

Sophia is a divine spirit devoted
to the good of all living souls.

Ecclesiastes
2:12-22

I began my contemplation of Sophia
by comparing Sophia, madness and folly.
I perceived that Sophia is more valuable
and more beneficial than folly;
As light is more valuable and more
beneficial than darkness.

The fool walks in darkness and obscurity.
The wise have eyes that see the light.

Yet I saw that both the wise
and the fool are destined
to the same death.

So I lamented and said to myself,
I will also suffer the fate of the fool.
For what reason, have I to be wise?
What is the meaning of life?

Why should I spend my life
searching for Sophia?
Even this search for Sophia,
I said to myself, is vanity.

The wise are remembered
no longer than the fool.
For as the passing days multiply,
all are forgotten.
At last, I observed,
the wise and the fool
die the same death!

What good is Sophia then?
I found no answer;
so I came to hate life.
Everything that was to be done
here on earth, under the sun,
was stress and strain,
a burden and a drudgery to me.

Emptiness was all around me and
it seemed, as if, I was chasing the wind.
I came to hate everything about my life
here on earth, under the sun,
since I would labor in vain and have
to leave the wealth of my existence
to my successors.

What sort of character will they have,
those that will succeed me?
Who knows whether they will be wise,
one with Sophia, or a fool?
Yet whatever they are,
they will be the authority
and heir of all the wealth of
my labor in this world.

Why should they inherit all that
another has acquired?
This is vanity and despair.

Ecclesiastes
2:22–25

What is the reward for us?
What is the reward for all of our labor,
our seeking, our striving, our struggles
to be wise and just, here under the sun?

All life long our mission on earth
seems to be pain and anger;
even at night,
the mind knows no peace.
This too is absurd.

There is nothing better than to eat
and drink and enjoy oneself
in return for all one's labors.
Yet I realized that this comes
as a gift from God.
For without God,

who can enjoy their food,
or who can be anxious?

James
4:14

Otherwise you do not know
what will come tomorrow.
For what is your life,
a bubble, that appears for awhile
then disappears?

Ecclesiastes
2:26

God gives Sophia
and knowledge and joy
to those who please him.
While to others is given only
the task of gathering and amassing
worldly wealth that can only be handed
over to someone else who pleases God.
This too is vanity and chasing the wind.

Ecclesiastes
8:1

Who is wise enough for all of this?
Who really knows the meaning of life,
of anything?

Job
4:21

How much longer will men die,
vanish forever, without even seeking Sophia?

Job
3:20-23

Why is light given to those
who live in misery?
Why is life given to those
who remain bitter in their souls?
They actually long for a death
that does not come, and seek death,
as if, it were a hidden treasure.

They rejoice and are exceedingly glad
when they can find their graves.
Why is light given to those
who are disappointed in God?

Ecclesiasticus
2:14

The heavy heart of bitterness
befalls you who have given up the quest!
What will you do when your Lord calls you?

Job
3:24-26

Personally, I cannot eat without sighing;
and groans pour out of me like floods.
The things that I have feared the most,
have come upon me.
I know no peace, no safety,
no rest, no quiet; only troubles.

Job
11:7

So, I asked:
"Can one by searching find God?"

Job
28:12

Where then can Sophia be found?

Job
28:14-20

The depth said,
"Sophia is not in me:"
The sea said,
"Sophia is not in me."

Sophia cannot be bought with gold.
Sophia is worth more than silver.
Neither gold nor jewels can equal
the value of Sophia:
the worth of Sophia is greater than these.

Tell me, then, I asked;
"How and where will I find Sophia?"

Job
28:22-23

Death and destruction said
that they had heard with their own ears,
the fame of Sophia. They said:
"Only God knows the way to Sophia
and how to become wise!"

Proverbs
1:7; 9-10; 15:33
Psalms
111:10
Job
28:28

And God said:
"Sophia?
The reverence and love of God is
the beginning of Sophia."

Job
11:5-6

O, if only God would speak to you.
Open his lips and tell you,
and show you the secrets of Sophia.
That her secrets are greater
than anything that is!

Job
32:7-8

I said, Days should speak, and
the multitude of acquired years
should teach individuals about Sophia.

There is a sacred feminine spirit
in all individuals;
the inspiration of the All-knowing
makes them wise.

James
1:5–6

If any of you seek, desire, or lack Sophia,
ask of God, that gives with open arms
to all that ask, and Sophia shall be given
to you, shall be known to you.

But ask with sincerity in Faith.

Hebrews
11:1

Now Faith is the promise of things
hoped for, the proof of things not seen.

Hebrews
11:13

Many of God's friends and holy prophets
have died in Faith.
Not having actually received the promises,
not having seen the proof of them,
but being assured of them,

and this assurance convinced and persuaded them,
embraced and loved them, and helped them
accept that they were pilgrims on the earth.

Ecclesiasticus
51:9

Thus, I did send a prayer up from the earth.
And I begged to be saved from death.

Ecclesiasticus
51:13

Frankly, I asked specifically
for Sophia in my prayers.

Ecclesiasticus
51:20

I set my heart on being endowed with Sophia.

Ecclesiasticus
51:22

With Sophia comes the advantage of being
enhanced with understanding
from the beginning.

Ecclesiasticus
51:27

See for yourself what small price
I have paid, compared to the great
wealth and noble peace, I have found.

Ecclesiasticus
24:1–2

Listen to the good words and blessings
of Sophia, from her own mouth,
as she speaks, worthy of praise
and adoration among her people,
in the presence of the Most High and
in the gathering of the heavenly host:

Ecclesiasticus
24:3-4

"I am the Word
which came from the mouth of the Most High.
Like a fine mist,
I embrace and softly cover the whole earth.
The sanctum of my home was in heaven;
my throne was in a culmination of clouds.
Alone I did circle the sky and
pass through the depths of the abyss."

Ecclesiasticus
24:6

"The waves of the sea, the whole earth,
and every people and nation
were in my influence and power."

Ecclesiasticus
24:19

"Come and draw near to me, you who love me;
and live on my wealth."

Ecclesiasticus
24:9

"Before the beginning of time, I was;
and I shall remain forevermore."

Ecclesiasticus
24:32-33

"I will fulfill my prophesy of peace
and bequeath it to all future generations.
Once again I will make peace shine
brighter than the dawn, and
not one will not see the light."

Ecclesiasticus
24:28-29

No man has ever completely known Sophia.
From the first man to the modern man,
not one has been able to explain or
solve her mystery completely.
For her thoughts are greater than the ocean
and her intent is greater than any abyss.

James
3:13

Who is wise and enlightened and endowed
with the knowledge of light among you?
Let them express with words of Wisdom
their works with the serenity of Sophia.

James
3:17

Sophia is holy, is divine, is pure,
is peaceable, is gentle.
Sophia is filled with compassion.
Happiness comes to you when Sophia
is called by prayers with sincerity and love.

Ecclesiastes
9:1

I applied my mind to all this.
I understood that the wise are
bound together in the love of God.

(The Book of Wisdom)
The Wisdom of Solomon
8:16

With Sophia in my heart, I find peace.
There is no conflict with Sophia.
When Sophia shares my life with me,
there is no pain.
With Sophia, I know only gladness and joy.

Job
4:6

Does your religion, your faith,
your piety give you encouragement,
comfort, confidence, guidance?
Does your way of life give you hope?

Ephesians 1:16
Philippians 1:3
Colossians 1:3
I Thessalonians 1:2

Everyday I make mention of you in my prayers.
Because of your love,
I give thanks for you,
unceasingly, in my prayers.

Psalms
55:17

Evening, morning and at noon I pray,
unceasingly, I pray.

Ephesians
4:3

Endeavouring to keep the oneness of the spirit
in the circle of Love and Peace and Wisdom.

Jude
1:21

Keep yourselves always in the love of God.

Ephesians
5:9

You are the light.

Ephesians
6:23-24

Peace, Love, Wisdom, Faith, Grace and
Immortality are yours.

Ephesians
2:17

Proclaim the good news!
Peace to you!

Book III

Blessings of Sophia

Ephesians
3:7

I was made a minister, by God's gift
of Sophia.
Bestowed, unmerited on me
in the working of his power.

Proverbs
4:4

My children,
let your hearts treasure these words:

Ephesians
2:22

You are being built into a
spiritual dwelling for God.

Ephesians
5:18

Let the Holy Spirit fill you.

Ephesians
4:23

You will be made new in mind and spirit.

Ephesians
5:4

Be thanking God.

Ephesians
1:18

That your inward eyes may be illumined.

Colossians
2:2–3

That your hearts might be comforted
and bound together with the promise of love
and peace that comes with the riches
that Sophia brings.

That your hearts might know and understand
the secret of God; in whom all
the treasures of Sophia abound.

Ecclesiasticus
6:22

Sophia is entitled to the divine right
of her name, for she approaches the elect.

Proverbs
4:7

Sophia is the guiding spirit;
therefore seek Sophia;
and in all your seeking,
you will become wise.

Ecclesiasticus
4:11–12

Sophia elevates her children to honor.
Sophia has the tender passion
of a mother's love for those who seek her.

All those who love Sophia love life;
to begin immediately to be her disciple
is to be filled with happiness and joy.

Ecclesiasticus
4:13

All those who attain Sophia
will rise to majestic fame;
they will walk in the light
with the blessings of the Lord.

Ecclesiasticus
4:14–15

All those who become her disciples
serve the Holy One.
The Lord loves those who love Sophia.

Ecclesiasticus
4:16

To all those who have faith in Sophia;
she will be their heritage and
the inheritance of their children.

Ecclesiasticus
4:17–18

At first as she leads you on the way
of transformation, through your doubts
and fears; her complexity might baffle you,
until you trust her with all of your heart.
Then she will approach you and fill you
with happiness as she reveals her secrets to
you.

Ecclesiasticus
4:19

But if you alter your course and deviate
from her ways, she will abandon you
in the next world.

Ecclesiasticus
6:18

My children, seek the holy order of Sophia
while you are young, and she will remain
with you until your hair is white.

Ecclesiasticus
6:19

Cultivate her like the farmer cultivates
the fields, and reap her generous harvest.
You will work a little while, but it will
not be long before you are eating her fruits.

Ecclesiasticus
6:20

How arrogant she is to the ignorant.
The fool cannot endure her;
like a heavy stone she encumbers him,
and quickly, he pushes her away.

Proverbs
27:3

A stone is heavy, but the bitterness
of a fool is heavier still.

Proverbs
13:9

The light of the wise shines forever.

Proverbs
16:32

More power has a person of Wisdom
than one who rules a city.

Ecclesiasticus
6:27–28

Invite Sophia into your life now,
and she will come to you.
Once you follow her, at no time,

let her go.
In the end you will find the peace
she gives; Sophia will become a
delight and joy to you.

Proverbs
24:13–14

My children, eat the honey, that is good;
and as the honeycomb sweetens your lips,
so shall the knowledge of Sophia
sweeten your souls.

Once you have found Sophia,
you will know Immortality and Eternal Peace.

Proverbs
16:16

Better the gain of Sophia than gold!

Ecclesiastes
7:12

For Sophia is an answer,
and money is an answer;
but the value of the knowledge of Sophia
is Sophia gives eternal life
to those that know her and love her.

Ecclesiastes
7:11

Sophia is generous with her blessings;
and those that see the light of the sun
inherit her abundance.

Proverbs
8:35

Sophia says:
"Whoever discovers me,
discovers the essence of life,
and shall receive all the
blessings of the Lord."

Proverbs
16:7

If your ways please the Lord,
he will make even your enemies
to be at peace with you.

Ecclesiasticus
6:14-16

A faithful friend is a safe sanctuary;
whoever finds one has found a unique
treasure.
A faithful friend is priceless;
their worth is beyond measure.

A faithful friend is an elixir
of life, and all those with a reverence
and love for God find such a friend.
They love others and themselves.

(The Book of Wisdom)
The Wisdom of Solomon
5:12-14

As an arrow is shot at its destination,
the parting of the air is not seen,
and one does not know where
the arrow has gone through.

So is our life;
we are barely born and before we know it,
we cease to be.

Does our life show the path of peace
or destruction?

The hope of the godless is like
the leaf in the storm, like the flurry
of smoke that the wind scatters,
like the memory of a one-day guest,
soon forgotten.

(The Book of Wisdom)
The Wisdom of Solomon
5:15–20

But noble souls live forever;
their reward and appreciation
comes from the Most High.

The Most High keeps them safe in his care.
They shall receive the royal crown of
glory and beauty,
a gift from the hand of the Lord himself.

He will keep them safe with his right hand,
and protect them with his arm.
He will put his love on for armour,
and make creation transform his enemies.

He will wear the armour of justice
on his breast, and his helmet shall be
his jugdment; holiness will be his shield,
and all the world will unite with
him and Sophia.

(The Book of Wisdom)
The Wisdom of Solomon
6:1-3

Listen now, you who have the governing
power of authority.
Be wise and take caution.
Hear these words.

(The Book of Wisdom)
The Wisdom of Solomon
6:9

I speak to you that you might know Sophia,
and not lead your people to destruction, but
live in peace and prosperity with Sophia.

(The Book of Wisdom)
The Wisdom of Solomon
5:21-23

There is a power greater than your authority
that will strike like a bolt of lightning,
upon those who do not honor Sophia.

If any of you who govern nations
appreciate your positions, it is time
now for you to honor Sophia.

(The Book of Wisdom)
The Wisdom of Solomon
7:14

Sophia is an inexhaustible treasure to all.
Those who acknowledge and love her
become God's friends, exalted to him
through her teachings.

1 John
4:1

Beloved, believe not every spirit,
but try the spirits whether they are of God;
because many false prophets
go out into the world.
Seek Sophia, so that you can
discern the spirits.

St. John
1:23

In the words of the prophet Isaiah, I said:
I am a voice crying out in the wilderness,
crying:

Ephesians
1:17

That God, the Father of glory,
may give to you,
the spirit of Sophia.

St. Mark
14:38

Truly, the spirit is ready,
but the flesh is weak.

I Corinthians
1:10

Now, brothers and sisters,
I beseech you,
by the name of our Lord,
Jesus Christ, that you all agree,
and that there be no divisions
among you; but that you be
perfectly joined together
in heart and mind.

I Corinthians
1:13

Is the symbol of Christ divided?

I Corinthians
2:7

But we speak the Wisdom
of God in a mystery,
even the secret of Sophia,
which God has given to us
for our glory.

I Corinthians
2:12

Now we are speaking of,
not the spirit of this world,
but the spirit which is of God.

I Corinthians
4:20

For the kingdom of God
is not in word, but in power.

I Corinthians
4:21

What is your desire?
That I come to you with a rod,
or in love, and in the spirit
of Sophia?

I Corinthians
2:1–3

My brothers and sisters,
I come to you with love and
the truth of God.
And I try to make sure that
I do not think about anything,
except Jesus Christ, crucified.

I Corinthians
2:8

If any of the princes of this world
knew Sophia, they would not have
crucified the Lord of glory.

I Corinthians
2:4

I stand before you weak,
and trembling with fear,
praying that you understand that the words,
I speak to you,

are not enticing words of
worldly wisdom, but the
words of Sophia of
the Spirit of God.

I Corinthians
2:6–7

I speak words to move you.
Those that are wise understand the words,
for they understand we are speaking not
of the wisdom of this world,
of some passing age.

We are speaking of Sophia,
an inexhaustible spiritual power,
impervious to time, that is,
will be and has always been with God.

I Corinthians
2:9

It is written:
Eyes have not seen,
nor have ears heard,
nor have hearts imagined
the wonders that God
has prepared for those
that love him.

I Corinthians
2:12

Now we are receiving
the Spirit of God in Sophia.

I Corinthians
4:5

My judge is the Lord.

Exodus
3:14

And God said,
I AM THAT I AM.

Exodus
31:1–3

And the Lord said,
"I have filled them with the
Spirit of God, in Sophia."

Genesis
1:2

And the Spirit of God
moved upon the face of the waters.

Genesis
2:4

In the day that God made the earth,
the heavens, and
every plant of the field.

Proverbs
3:19

The Lord with Sophia
by his side has founded the earth;
and has established the heavens
with this understanding.

Proverbs
3:17–18

All the paths of Sophia are Peace.
She is a tree of life
to those that find her;
and happy is everyone
that loves her.

Proverbs
3:16

Long life is in her right hand;
and in her left hand
are riches and honor.

Book IV

Uniting Power of Sophia

Proverbs
8:12

"I am Sophia."

Proverbs
3:14–15

To the wise, Sophia is
more treasured than any jewel;
of all the things that can be
desired on earth, there is
nothing worth more than Sophia.

Proverbs
7:4

Call Sophia your sister.
Say to Sophia, you are my sister.
My sister Sophia.

(The Book of Wisdom)
The Wisdom of Solomon
7:6

For all of us,
there is one solitary way into life
one solitary way out of life.

(The Book of Wisdom)
The Wisdom of Solomon
7:7–8

For this reason I prayed
and I was given understanding;
I offered up prayers and
the Spirit of Sophia came to me.
I love Sophia more than sceptre
and throne; and I considered
riches as nothing compared to her.

(The Book of Wisdom)
The Wisdom of Solomon
7:10–14

I loved Sophia more than beauty or health.
I loved Sophia more than the light of day,

because her light is radiance that never
sleeps.

In her presence all good things came to me,
for in her hands are infinite riches.
I loved all the gifts Sophia gave me,
but at the time, I still did not know her
as, the Mother of Life.

I share this with you,
all of this newly acquired knowledge
and understanding, so that you too
can know that Sophia is an inexhaustible
treasure for the world.
For all those who know and love Sophia
will become God's friends.

(The Book of Wisdom)
The Wisdom of Solomon
7:21

All of this, the secret and the obvious,
I have learned because Sophia
was my teacher;
Sophia, the Mother of All.

(The Book of Wisdom)
The Wisdom of Solomon
7:22–24

Sophia is a holy Spirit.
Sophia is unique, intelligent, light-giving,
diverse, energy, pathos, feeling, guardian.

Sophia is comforter, kind, active,
benevolent, beneficent, omnipotent,
unchanging, ever-present.

Sophia is peace, all-loving, all-wise, all-
knowing, entering and filling all intelligent,
pure and beautiful spirits of light.

Sophia transforms.
Sophia is so pure that she flows,
pervading and permeating all things.

(The Book of Wisdom)
The Wisdom of Solomon
7:25–26

Sophia is the inspiration of the
power of God, the true and pure

out-pouring of his glory.
Nothing that is not pure can enter her.

Sophia is the idea of eternal light.
Sophia is the perfect reflection
of God's image and power of goodness.

Proverbs
1:1–7

The proverbs of Solomon
the son of David, king of Israel:

To know Sophia and her teachings;
to know she speaks words of understanding.

To receive the holy order of Sophia,
justice and equity;
to give subtlety to the simple,
to give knowledge and choice to the young.

The wise will hear,
and will increase their learning;
the wise will attain wise counsel.

To understand a proverb,
and the interpretation.
To understand the words of the wise
and their sayings.

The beginning, the first step
to understanding Sophia
is to love God.

(The Book of Wisdom)
The Wisdom of Solomon
7:27–28

Complete in her oneness,
united in her completeness,
altogether, indivisible,
Sophia can do any and all things.

Herself, unchanging,
she can change all things;
she makes all things new.

Sophia appears to the elect.
She lives in the holy souls

of all ages and makes them wise:
God's friends and holy prophets.

Those that live with the peace
of Love and Wisdom
are blessed.
God loves those that live with Sophia.

(The Book of Wisdom)
The Wisdom of Solomon
7:29

Her radiance is more dazzling than
the noonday sun, and
the magnificence of her light outshines
all of the constellations.

Sophia is the light above all lights.
For the light of day surrenders
to the darkness of night,
but the light of Sophia
is impenetrable and indisoluble.

(The Book of Wisdom)
The Wisdom of Solomon
7:30

Sophia has the power to unite the world;
to pervade and permeate all hearts
with the inner light of love.

(The Book of Wisdom)
The Wisdom of Solomon
8:1

I love Sophia.
I have searched for her
all the days of my life.
I have longed and aspired
to be one with her.

(The Book of Wisdom)
The Wisdom of Solomon
8:2–3

I fell in love with her beauty.
There is not one who has seen her

that has not fallen in love with her
beauty, her radiance, her harmony.

Her nearness, her proximity to God,
is in accord with the magnificence
of her noble beginning:

Sophia is loved by the God of Love.
Sophia is loved by the God of All.
God loves Sophia.

(The Book of Wisdom)
The Wisdom of Solomon
8:3–4

Truly, Sophia is co-eternal,
co-existing with God.

Sophia is the teacher
that can resolve the mysteries
of God's knowledge.
For God confers with Sophia
on all he is to do.

(The Book of Wisdom)
The Wisdom of Solomon
8:5-9

If life is to be an acquisition of wealth,
who holds greater wealth than Sophia,
who is co-creator of all things?

If life is to be a challenge of the intellect,
who holds greater Wisdom than Sophia, herself,
who is Wisdom?

If life is a love and quest for Truth,
why, Truth is one of the gifts of Sophia.

Sophia teaches the way to self-knowledge.
Sophia is the inspiration of genius.
Sophia is harmony and peace.
Sophia is courage and strength in serenity.

Of all the things needed in life,
what is of more value than these?

If life is an adventure of great experience,
Sophia knows the past.
Sophia can predict the future.

Sophia knows what has happened and
what will be.

Sophia can interpret oracles and
solve riddles and mysteries.
Sophia has foreknowledge of omens and signs.

Sophia has foresight of miracles and wonders,
of beginnings and conclusions,
of this age and all ages.

Thus, it was that I resolved;
that I set my heart,
on having Sophia come into my life;
and live my life with me.

Knowing she would counsel me
in prosperity and good times.
Knowing she would comfort me
in grief and troubled times.

(The Book of Wisdom)
The Wisdom of Solomon
8:13

By the grace of Sophia,
I shall know Immortality,
and shall leave the sustaining
and unforgotten memory of Sophia
to all those who follow me.

(The Book of Wisdom)
The Wisdom of Solomon
8:16

With Sophia in my heart,
I shall know Love;
for where Sophia reigns
there is no bitterness.

With Sophia in my heart,
I shall know Peace;
for where Sophia reigns
there is no conflict or pain.

With Sophia in my heart,
I shall know Happiness;
for where Sophia reigns
there is only gladness and joy.

(The Book of Wisdom)
The Wisdom of Solomon
6:12–17

Sophia is luminous light
and never grows dim.
Sophia appears and is easily
seen by those who love her.

Sophia is found
by those who seek her.

Sophia is able to foresee those
who desire her so she makes
herself known to them.

Seek Sophia now and
you will always overcome adversity;
you will find her
waiting for you.

Just thinking about her
brings understanding.
Hope for Sophia and expect her
to be with you.
Just think of her and
pain and fear will automatically
leave you.

Sophia wanders the earth
looking for you, who are
deserving of her.

In soft-hearted graciousness,
she will appear to you as you go;
coming to meet you in
your every thought.

(The Book of Wisdom)
The Wisdom of Solomon
8:17–18

In my inner thoughts and
in the depths of my heart,
I did understand and know:

that the loving existence
with Sophia brings immortality;
that pure peace comes with
the friendship of her love;
that inexhaustible riches come
from working for her in the
cultivation of her holy order
of Wisdom.

(The Book of Wisdom)
The Wisdom of Solomon
8:19–20

I searched the world over
looking for Sophia,
asking and wondering,
how I could unite with her.
How I might become wise.
And then I realized it was a paradox:

One must ask
for Wisdom.
But one must have
Wisdom to know for what
to ask.

And it was an indication
of the beginning of Wisdom
to understand from where
Sophia comes.

(The Book of Wisdom)
The Wisdom of Solomon
8:20

Seeing and understanding this,
I did kneel and bow my head
in sacred awe and with all
my heart and soul, I prayed:

(The Book of Wisdom)
The Wisdom of Solomon
9:1-4

God, of our fathers,
give us Wisdom
who sits beside thy throne.

Send her down from the holy heavens
that we might understand

the true meaning of Love,
and fulfill our dreams of
Peace on Earth.

That the old order of
death, mourning, crying and pain
might end.

That we may always hold bright
the promise of a new beginning.

Revelation
22:17

And the Spirit and the bride (Sophia)
say, "Come!"
Let each who hear say, "Come!"
All who wish to accept the
drink of immortality, Come!

Revelation
22:12

"Behold, I come now!"

Revelation
22:13

"I am Alpha and Omega,
the first and the last,
the beginning and the end."

Revelation
21:1

Truly, I saw a new heaven and a new earth:
for the first heaven and earth
existed no more.

Revelation
21:2

I saw the holy city, New Jerusalem,
coming down from heaven,

coming down from God.
Elaborate and beautiful,
as a bride adorned for
her husband.

Revelation
21:10

Here is Sophia!

Revelation
21:23

The new city has no need of
the light of the sun
nor the moon to shine in it;
for the glory of God—Sophia—
did lighten it!

Revelation
21:3

I heard a great voice
out of heaven saying:

Revelation
21:3–5

"Behold,
God and Sophia are with you.
You are the children of Light.
Every tear will be wiped
from your eyes.

There shall be no more death;
nor sorrow, nor crying, nor pain,
for the holy order of Sophia
is here.
Behold, all things are made new!
Behold, A New Beginning!"

*This is one beginning of the divine
validation of Sophia, the dawn of light that
renews the living soul of mankind. As a holy
spirit that lives within, Sophia lovingly
transforms energy making known the Spirit of
Wisdom as separate and one with the Spirit of
Love. Lovers of Wisdom know the union with
Sophia to be the great calmness of mind and
heart known as the philosopher's noble peace.*

*Glory gives the Light and the Light cannot
be contained. The Father of Love and the
Children of Love hold reverent the Mother of
the Light of Life and the world-wide
Renaissance is Peace.*

*Peace begins in You. It is a simple formula.
It is a divine task.*

*It is a divine task for you to be a torch-
bearer; to ignite and keep aflame, even a tiny
flicker of Hope that the world might attain
Peace.*

It is a divine task for you, for one heart to be free, frees all other hearts with a connecting link of Love.

It is a divine task for you to aspire to walk the path of the wise, to know Love, and to Love Wisdom.

It is a divine task for you to fulfill the prophesy of Peace on Earth.

It is a divine task that will be; for it is written:

The Second Paradise Will Come in You.